to:_____

from:_____

LIFE WITH DAD

DEDICATION

Dedicated in loving memory to my dad, Julius "Jay" Decetis,
whose dry stoic sense of humor and committed discipline
kept me from incarceration.

Published by Sellers Publishing, Inc.
161 John Roberts Road, South Portland, ME 04106
Visit us at www.sellerspublishing.com • E-mail: rsp@rsvp.com

Copyright © 2015 Sellers Publishing, Inc.
Cartoons copyright © 2015 Eric Decetis

ISBN-13: 978-1-4162-4548-3

Printed and bound in China.

10 9 8 7 6 5 4 3 2

LIFE WITH DAD

CARTOONS BY ERIC DECETIS

SELLERS

PUBLISHING

Dad always thought laughter was the best medicine. . . .

—JACK HANDEY

Daughters always have a special place in Dad's heart.

The place of the father in the modern suburban family is a very small one, particularly if he plays golf.

—BERTRAND RUSSELL

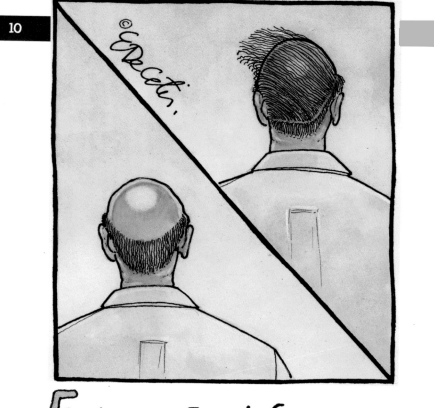

Extreme Dad Comb-Over

Any man can be a father, but it
takes someone special to be a dad.
—PROVERB

A boy's father is his king.

—RABBI ELIEZER

To a father, nothing is more
sweet than a daughter.

—EURIPIDES

Being a great father is like shaving. No matter how good you shaved today, you have to do it again tomorrow.

—REED MARKHAM

©E De Cetis.
Look Dad! I made potty all by myself!
MAX
You sure did, Billy. You... sure... did.
Grrrrrr

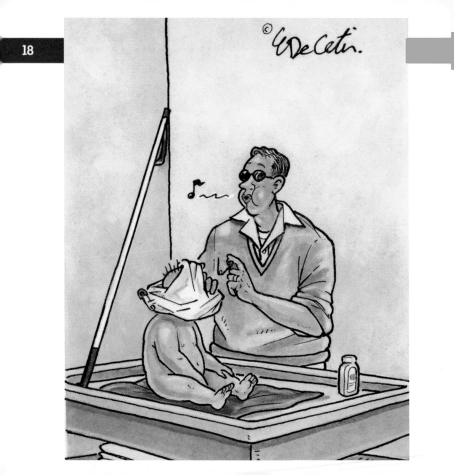

Men should always change diapers. It's a very rewarding experience. It's mentally cleansing. It's like washing dishes, but imagine if the dishes were your kids, so you really love the dishes.

—CHRIS MARTIN

There is no such thing as fun for the whole family.

—JERRY SEINFELD

EDeCetis.©
Honest, D-D-Dad. My report card's "in the cloud."
Yeah? So's your allowance.

Children are a great comfort in your old age. And they help you reach it faster too.

—LIONEL KAUFFMAN

There are times when fatherhood seems like nothing more than feeding the hand that bites you.

Fatherhood is pretending the
present you love most is
soap-on-a-rope.

—BILL COSBY

People who love to eat are always
the best people.

—JULIA CHILD

Having a staring contest with a newborn is one of the weirdest things you'll ever do. And it is highly recommended.

—ROSS MCCAMMON

My father had a profound influence on me.
He was a lunatic.

—SPIKE MILLIGAN

My dad had no special talents, but he did love his dog.

Sometimes dads are just winging this fathering thing.

Dad, how come you signed my report card with an "X"?
I don't want your teacher to think a kid with grades this bad...
...could possibly have a father who could read or write.
© DeCet.

Dad's great about showing us how to do stuff. Even if he doesn't really know what he's doing, he passes that knowledge on to us.

—DAVID BUTLER

Good ole Dad — always looking
on the bright side.

©Grzelak.
Nice work, son. You missed the car, but you nailed his bald spot.

If the new American father feels
bewildered and even defeated,
let him take comfort from the
fact that whatever he does in any
fathering situation, it has a 50
percent chance of being right.

—BILL COSBY

Nobody ever said that a dad's job was easy.

Who needs Superman when you
have a dad?

Every father should remember that
one day his son will follow his example
instead of his advice.
—CHARLES F. KETTERING

Fatherhood is great because you can ruin
someone from scratch.

—JON STEWART

When I was a baby, my father used to throw me up in the air and then asnwer the phone.

—RITA RUDNER

I love the comic opportunities
that come up in the context of a
father-son relationship.

—HARRISON FORD

When I was a kid, I said to my
father one afternoon, "Daddy,
will you take me to the zoo?"
He answered, "If the zoo wants you,
let them come and get you."

—JERRY LEWIS

Honest, Dad, somethin's wrong with the lawn mower.
You look fine to me. When you finish the lawn and pullin' weeds, feel free to wash the car and paint the house.
P.O.
© EDeCosta.

My Father loved people, children,
and pets.

—TONY VISCONTI

I'm a fun father, but not a good father. The hard decisions always went to my wife.

—JOHN LITHGOW

You know, fathers just have a way
of putting everything together.
　　　　　　　　　—ERIKA COSBY